STEFAN WOLPE

G000124738

FORM IV:
BROKEN SEQUENCES

Piano

duration: 4 minutes

C. F. PETERS CORPORATION

NEW YORK   -   LONDON   -   FRANKFURT

for Robert Miller

FORM IV. BROKEN SEQUENCES

Stefan Wolpe
(in his 67th year)
1969

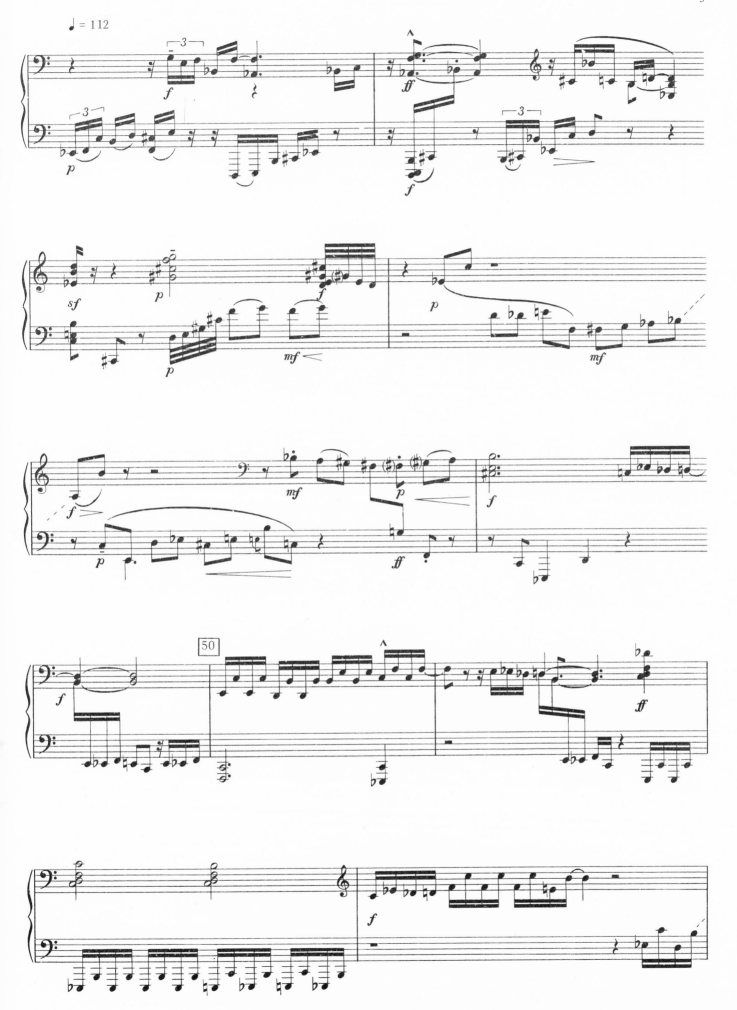

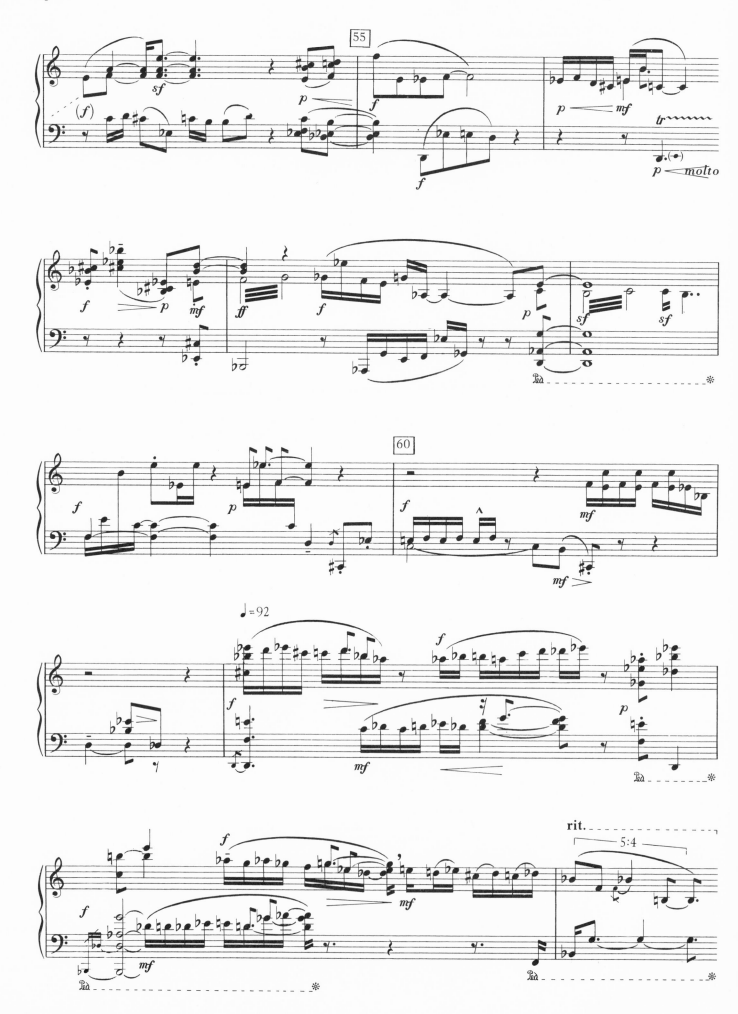

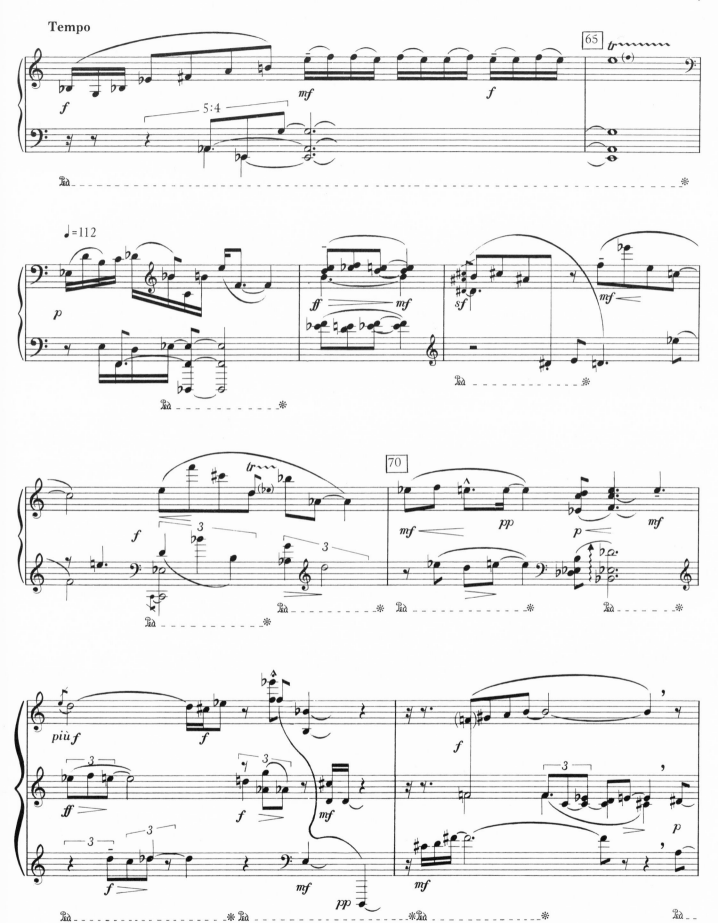

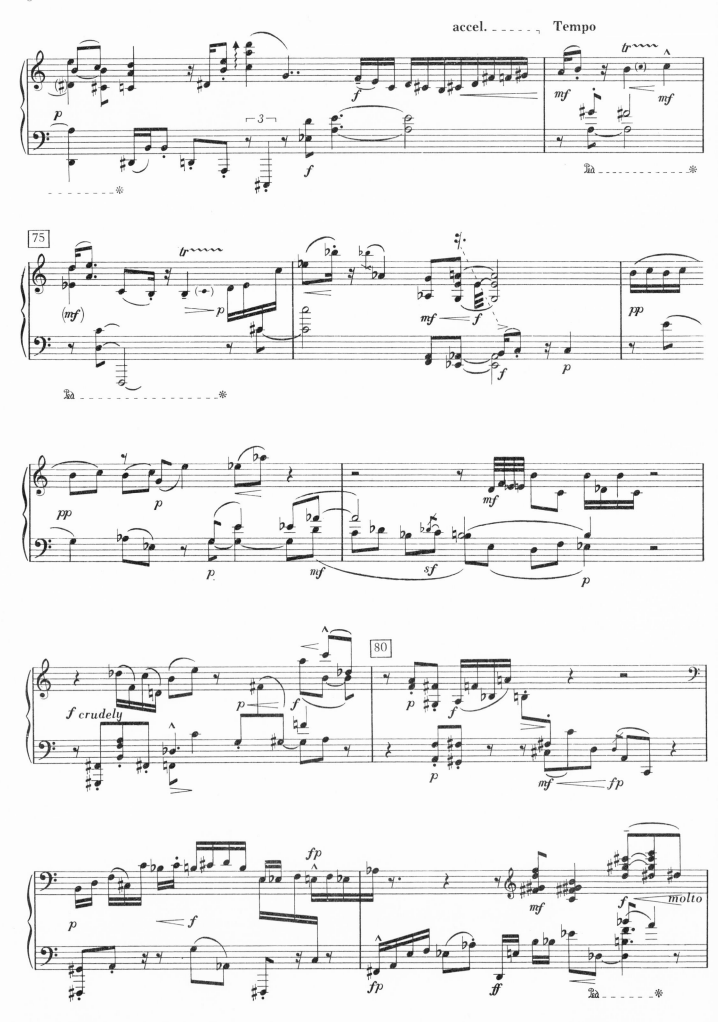

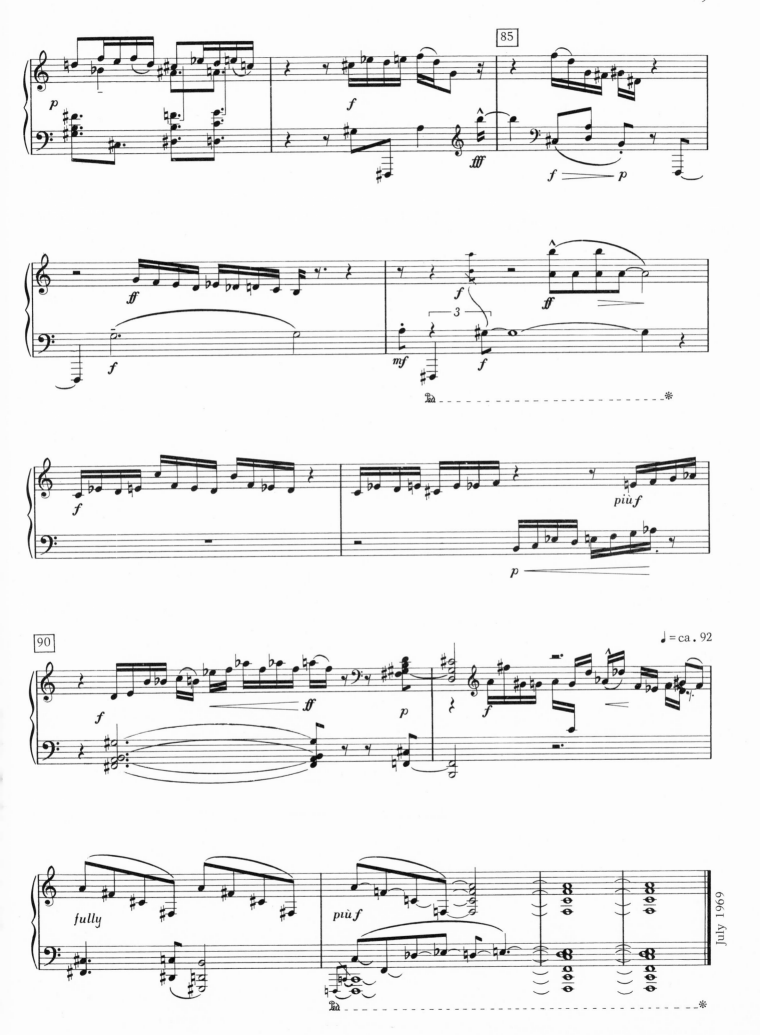

July 1969